W9-ABH-044

WITHDRAWN
R COLLEGE LIBRARY

Date Due

Dec 6 38			
Nov 2 '40			
Mar 24 '4?			
1930A M			
May 8 '56			

Library Bureau Cat. no. 1137

THE COMING VICTORY
OF DEMOCRACY

TRANSLATED FROM THE GERMAN BY
AGNES E. MEYER

THE COMING VICTORY

OF DEMOCRACY

by

THOMAS MANN

1 9 **1938** 3 8

NEW YORK

ALFRED A KNOPF

COPYRIGHT *1938 by Alfred A. Knopf, Inc. All rights reserved. No part of this book may be reproduced in any form without permission in writing from the publisher, except by a reviewer who may quote brief passages in a review to be printed in a magazine or newspaper. Manufactured in the United States of America.*

PUBLISHED JUNE 20, 1938
SECOND PRINTING, JULY 1938
THIRD PRINTING, AUGUST 1938
FOURTH PRINTING, OCTOBER 1938

320.4
M31c

THE COMING VICTORY
OF DEMOCRACY

*is the text of the lecture which, in slightly
abbreviated form, was delivered by Thomas
Mann on his coast-to-coast lecture tour
February to May 1938.*

159135

THE EXPRESSION " to carry owls to Athens " is a familiar humanistic figure of speech in Germany. It denotes an act of superfluous effort, the transfer of an article to a place where such things already exist in abundance. As the owl was the sacred bird of Athena, owls were numerous in Athens and anyone who felt obliged to increase their number would have exposed himself to ridicule.

In undertaking to speak on democracy in America, ladies and gentlemen, I feel as if I, too, were carrying owls to Athens. It looks as if I were not aware that I am in the classic land of democracy, where the mode of thought and the type of social structure which are characterized by this name are

essentially at home and a universally ingrained con-
viction; where, in short, democracy is an all-pre-
vailing matter of course, upon which the American
needs no instruction — least of all from a European. On the contrary, Europe has had much to
learn from America as to the nature of democracy.
It was your American statesmen and poets such as
Lincoln and Whitman who proclaimed to the world
democratic thought and feeling, and the democratic
way of life, in imperishable words. The world has
probably never produced a master of words who has
known so well as Whitman how to elevate and translate a social principle such as democracy into in-
toxicating song, or how to endow it with such power-
ful emotional content, representing a magnificent
fusion of spirituality and sensuousness.

No, America needs no instruction in the things
that concern democracy. But instruction is one
thing — and another is memory, reflection, re-ex-
amination, the recall to consciousness of a spiritual
and moral possession of which it would be dangerous to feel too secure and too confident. No

worth-while possession can be neglected. Even physical things die off, disappear, are lost, if they are not cared for, if they do not feel the eye and hand of the owner and are lost to sight because their possession is taken for granted. Throughout the world it has become precarious to take democracy for granted — even in America; for America belongs to the cultural territory of the Occident and participates in its inner destiny, in the ups and downs of its spiritual and moral life. It cannot isolate itself therefrom. It is not easy to speak on the coming victory of democracy at a moment when the aggressive brutality of fascism seems to be so distressingly triumphant. The moment, indeed, does not seem to be well chosen, and *European* democracy at least in its moral weakness seems to forbid any optimistic prophecy. Even America feels today that democracy is not an assured possession, that it has enemies, that it is threatened from within and from without, that it has once more become a problem. America is aware that the time has come for democracy to take stock of itself, for recollection and restatement and conscious consideration, in a word, for its renewal in thought and feeling.

The advantage, or the apparent advantage, of the tendencies that are hostile to democracy is, above all, the charm of novelty — a charm to which humanity always shows itself highly susceptible. What Cæsar said of the ancient Gauls, that they were *novarum rerum cupidi,* eager for new things, is true of humanity as a whole — for reasons which tend to support a pessimistic-compassionate judgment concerning its destiny. For it is the fate of man in no condition and under no circumstances ever to be entirely at ease upon this earth; no form of life is wholly suitable nor wholly satisfactory to him. Why this should be so, why there should always remain upon earth for this creature a modicum of insufficiency, of dissatisfaction and suffering, is a mystery — a mystery that may be a very honourable one for man, but also a very painful one; in any case it has this consequence: that humanity, in small things as in great, strives for variety, change, for the new, because it promises him an amelioration and an alleviation of his eternally semi-painful condition.

I repeat: the greatest power, the essential fascination of the ideas and tendencies which threaten democracy today and render it problematical, is their charm of novelty. Upon this the fascists place their emphasis, of this they boast; their revolutionary demeanour, their attitude of youthfulness and opportunism, are meant to attract the youth of the world, and in Europe, at least, not infrequently succeed in doing so. In my opinion, youth is cheated when it surrenders to this fascination. Let me explain why this is so. I believe that the revolutionary opportunism and the glow of false dawn in these tendencies — it is obvious that I mean the fascist tendencies — are tainted magic. Not only in this respect, but particularly in this respect, fascism is so thoroughly false that honourable youth throughout the world should be ashamed to have anything to do with it. Moreover, susceptibility to it is not in the least a question of age or of youth. Older people are by no means excluded from this magic or invulnerable to it simply because they belong to another age and cannot keep up with the times and are thus obliged to leave this dew-drenched world of ideas, called fascism, to the young. For example, my great Norwegian colleague, Knut Hamsun, an already elderly man, is an ardent fascist. He gives active support to the fascist party in his own land and did not deny himself the satisfaction of openly ridiculing and insulting a world-famous victim of German fascism, the pacifist Ossietzky. However, this is not the conduct of an old man whose heart has remained particularly youthful but of a writer of the generation of 1870, upon whom Dostoyevsky and Nietzsche had a decisive literary influence. He has stuck fast in the movement of apostasy from liberalism generally characteristic of that period, without comprehending what is at stake today, and without realizing that he is hopelessly compromising his poetical genius through his political or, as I prefer to call it, his human behaviour. On the other hand, it can be established that the majority of youth throughout the world, in Europe and especially in America — indeed, it is safe to say the overwhelming majority

— will have nothing to do with what are called fascistic ideas, and are battling spiritually and even physically for entirely opposite ideals. Obviously the susceptibility to the fascist miasma has nothing to do with age or youth; it is much more a question of intelligence, of character, of the sense of truth, of human feeling; in short, the decisive factors are characteristics which belong or do not belong to age or to youth, and from this point of view decidedly nothing can be proved concerning the revolutionary prospects of fascism.

That does not prevent its shrill propaganda of youthfulness, its publicity tricks, from presenting democracy as decrepit, decayed, out of date, stale, and hopelessly tiresome, whereas it pictures itself as highly amusing and replete with life and future possibilities, as its well-known successes are supposed to prove to us. Daring and clever as fascism is in exploiting human weakness, it succeeds in meeting to some extent humanity's painful eagerness for novelty to which I have already alluded. And what seems to me necessary is that democracy should answer this fascist strategy with a rediscovery of itself, which can give it the same charm of novelty — yes, a much higher one than that which fascism seeks to exert. It should put aside the habit of taking itself for granted, of self-forgetfulness. It should use this wholly unexpected situation — the fact, namely, that it has again become problematical — to renew and rejuvenate itself by again becoming aware of itself. For democracy's resources of vitality and youthfulness cannot be overestimated; in comparison, the youthful insolence of fascism is a mere grimace. Fascism is a child of the times — a very offensive child — and draws whatever youth it possesses out of the times. But democracy is timelessly human, and timelessness always implies a certain amount of potential youthfulness, which need only be realized in thought and feeling in order to excel, by far, all merely transitory youthfulness in charms of every sort, in the charm of life and in the charm of beauty.

I called democracy timelessly human and fascism, its opponent, which today is so triumphantly asserting itself, a transitory manifestation. In doing so I am not forgetting that fascism also has deep

and perhaps indestructible roots in human nature;
for its essence is force. It is in physical and mental
oppression that fascism believes; this is what it prac-
tises, loves, honours, and glorifies. Oppression is
not only the ultimate goal but the first principle of
fascism, and we know only too well that force as a
principle is just as eternally human as its opposite,
the idea of justice. It is the stern fact-creating
principle. It can accomplish everything, or practically everything. Once it has subjugated the body
through fear, it can even subjugate thought. For
man in the long run cannot live a double life; in
order to live in harmony with himself, he adapts
his thoughts to the manner of life that force imposes
upon him. All this force can accomplish. Daily
we see justice grow pale before it and perish, because force is oppressive materialism and in the
field of experience is usually the victor, whereas justice is only an idea. But this " only," bitter and
pessimistic as it may sound, is nevertheless full
of pride and firmest confidence — confidence which
does not arise out of puerile and artificial idealism,
but is, on the contrary, based upon a greater knowl-

edge of the nature and reality of man than the only semi-intelligent belief in force.

For it is a singular thing, this human nature, and distinguished from the rest of nature by the very fact that it has been endowed with the idea, is dominated by the idea, and cannot exist without it, since human nature is what it is because of the idea. The idea is a specific and essential attribute of man, that which makes him human. It is within him a real and natural fact, so impossible of neglect that those who do not respect human nature's participation in the ideal — as force certainly does not — commit the clumsiest and, in the long run, the most disastrous mistakes. But the word " justice " is only one name for the idea — only one; there are other names which can be substituted that are equally strong, by no means lacking in vitality; on the contrary, even rather terrifying — for example, freedom and truth. It is impossible to decide which one should take precedence, which is the greatest. For each one expresses the idea in its totality, and one stands for the others. If we say *truth*, we also say *freedom* and *justice*; if we speak of freedom and justice, we mean truth. It is a complex of an indivisible kind, freighted with spirituality and elementary dynamic force. We call it the absolute. To man has been given the absolute — be it a curse or a blessing, it is a fact. He is pledged to it, his inner being is conditioned by it, and in the human sphere a force which is opposed to truth, hostile to freedom, and lacking in justice, acts in so low and contemptible a manner because it is devoid of feeling and understanding for the relationship between man and the absolute and without comprehension of the inviolable human dignity which grows out of this relationship.

You perceive, ladies and gentlemen, that I wish to give the word " democracy " a very broad meaning, a much broader one than the merely political sense of this word would suggest; for I am connecting it with the highest human attributes, with the idea and the absolute; I am relating it to the inalienable dignity of mankind, which no force, however humiliating, can destroy. This I must do if I am to fulfil the request which has been put to me — namely, to declare my faith in the ultimate victory of democracy over the tendencies and forces which threaten it today. If we only weigh one political system against another, of which one — namely, the hostile system — actually exhibits robust practical advantages over democracy, it is difficult to arrive at this faith. It must be founded upon the humanly timeless aspect of democracy, upon the unlimited powers of self-renewal which are its consequence, and upon its inexhaustible store of potential youthfulness, which is nourished by the absolute. For these are the qualities which make it possible for democracy to laugh at the boastful pretensions of the fascist dictatorships to youthfulness and future glory.

That this faith is connected with specific conditions whose historical fulfilment devolves upon democracy, I shall consider later. For the moment, I am concerned with a definition of democracy, and every definition of democracy is insufficient — insufficient for belief in it — if it is confined to the technical-political aspects. It is insufficient to define the democratic principle as the principle of majority rule and to translate democracy literally, all too literally, as government by the people, an expression of double meaning which could also signify mob rule, for that is more nearly the definition of fascism. It is even inadequate — correct as it may be — to reduce the democratic idea to the idea of peace, and to assert that the right of a free people to determine its own destiny includes respect for the rights of foreign people and thus constitutes the best guarantee for the creation of a community of nations and for peace. We must reach higher and envisage the whole. We must define democracy as that form of government and of society which is inspired above every other with the feeling and consciousness of the dignity of man.

The dignity of man — do we not feel alarmed and somewhat ridiculous at the mention of these words? Do they not savour of optimism grown feeble and stuffy — of after-dinner oratory, which scarcely harmonizes with the bitter, harsh, everyday truth about human beings? We know it — this truth. We are well aware of the nature of man, or, to be more accurate, the nature of men — and we are far from entertaining any illusions on the sub-

ject. The nature of man is transfixed in the sacred
words: " The imagination of man's heart is evil
from his youth." It has been described with philosophical cynicism in the phrase of Frederick II:
" the accursed race — *cette race maudite*." Yes,
yes, humanity — its injustice, malice, cruelty, its
average stupidity and blindness are amply demon-
strated, its egoism is crass, its deceitfulness, coward-
ice, its antisocial instincts, constitute our everyday
experience; the iron pressure of disciplinary con-
straint is necessary to keep it under any reasonable
control. Who cannot embroider upon the depravity
of this strange creature called man, who does not
often despair over his future or sympathize with
the contempt felt by the angels of heaven from the
day of creation for the incomprehensible interest
which the heavenly Father takes in this problematical creature? And yet it is a fact — more true today than ever — that we cannot allow ourselves, because of so much all too well-founded scepticism,
to despise humanity. Despite so much ridiculous
depravity, we cannot forget the great and the honourable in man, which manifest themselves as art

and science, as passion for truth, creation of beauty and the idea of justice; and it is also true that insensitiveness to the great mystery which we touch upon when we say " man " or " humanity " signifies spiritual death. That is not a truth of yesterday or the day before yesterday, antiquated, unattractive, and feeble. It is the new and necessary truth of today and tomorrow, the truth which has life and youth on its side in opposition to the false and withering youthfulness of certain theories and truths of the moment.

Did I say too much when I spoke of man as a great mystery? Whence does he come? From nature, animal nature, and thereby his conduct is unmistakably conditioned. But in him nature becomes conscious, it seems to have produced him not only to make him master over himself — that is merely the expression of something more profound; for in him nature opens a door to the spiritual, questions, admires, and judges itself in a being which belongs at the same time to itself and to a higher order of things. To become conscious means to acquire conscience, means the knowledge of what is good and what is evil. Nature that is infra-human does not know this difference. It is without guilt. In humanity nature becomes responsible. Man is nature's fall from grace, only it is not a fall, but just as positively an elevation as conscience is higher than innocence. What Christianity calls " original sin " is more than priestly trickery designed to suppress and control humanity — it is the deep feeling of man as a spiritual being for his natural infirmities and limitations, above which he raises himself through spirit. Is that infidelity to nature? By no means. It is according to nature's deepest intent. Because it is for its own spiritualization that nature produced mankind.

This dignity which the mysterious confers upon man, democracy recognizes and honours; democracy's understanding and respect for this quality, it calls " humanity." The anti-human, dictatorial mentality of our day ignores " original sin," or what may be called spiritual conscience. It considers the consciousness of sin, or spirituality, as injurious to military prowess. It teaches optimistic heroics — in direct and stupid contradiction of the extreme contempt for humanity, which it exalts in the same breath. For all men of violence, tyrants, those who seek to stupefy and stultify the masses, and all those who are intent upon turning a nation into an un-thinking war-machine in order to control free and thinking citizens — these necessarily despise humanity. They give the pretext, to be sure, that they wish to restore to mankind the honour which Christianity has sullied, by freeing him from original sin and forcing Germanic heroics down his throat. Under all circumstances they set themselves up as the leaders who have restored their country's honour. Even to Germany they have " restored its honour," if we are to believe their radio broadcasts. But in reality they practise a truly grotesque contempt of humanity — grotesque if we think of the victims, grotesque if we consider those who exercise the contempt, since they are themselves the most contempt-ible creatures.

I am willing to accept contempt which comes from on high, the contempt of the great personality that has outgrown ordinary human limitations. But it is impossible to understand how completely des-

picable creatures, lacking every moral and spiritual attribute, could undertake to be contemptuous.
It is, to be sure, the kind of contempt which strives
with all its might to degrade and corrupt humanity
in order to force the people to do its will. Terror
destroys people, that is clear. It corrupts character,
releases every evil impulse, turns them into cowardly hypocrites and shameless informers. It
makes them contemptible — that is the reason why
these contemners of humanity love terrorism. Their
delight in the abuse of people is dirty and pathologi-
cal. The treatment of the Jews in Germany, the concentration camps and the things which took place
and are still taking place in them, are the illustra-
tion and proof of this. Every kind of dishonour,
disgrace, ignominious distinctions such as the cut-
ting of the hair and the yellow spot, the compulsion
to moral suicide, the destruction of mind and soul
through bodily torture, the corruption of justice
through force until men, overcome by extreme hor-
ror, despair of justice and abjure it for the worship
of force — these are all expedients of this lust for
human degradation which it would be too much hon-

our to call devilish, for it is simply diseased. Can the flagrant actions which dictatorship permits itself be considered anything but diseased — the lies, the annihilation of truth, the deception — a deception so crass that it, too, amounts to violence? And is there not something diseased in the boundless confidence which the dictators place in a population that has been stultified and intellectually enfeebled to meet their desires and needs? There is but one public voice — theirs. Every other voice has been silenced. There is no contradiction, not even the slightest memory of opposition; they can say what they like. Undisturbed and to their heart's content they can crack the whip of lies over the heads of the populace — the whip of lies called propaganda.

Democracy, whatever may be its conception of humanity, has only the best of intentions toward it. Democracy wishes to elevate mankind, to teach it to think, to set it free. It seeks to remove from culture the stamp of privilege and disseminate it among the people — in a word, it aims at education. Education is an optimistic and humane concept; and respect for humanity is inseparable from it. Hostile

Thomas Mann

to mankind and contemptuous of it is the opposing concept called propaganda, which tries to stultify, stupefy, level, or regiment men for the purpose of military efficiency and, above all, to keep the dictatorial system in power. I do not wish to imply that propaganda could not be used in the sense of education — that is, in the democratic sense. It may be that all over the world and even in this country democracy has heretofore made too little use of it in its own educational sense. But certainly in the hands of the dictators propaganda is an instrument of cynical contempt for humanity.

Thus we see contradiction on both sides — apparently there is no escaping it in life. Democracy being a fertile ground for intellect and literature, for the perception of psychological truth and the search for it, contradicts itself inasmuch as it has an acute appreciation and makes a critical analysis of the comical wickedness of man, but nevertheless insists resolutely upon the dignity of man and the possibility of educating him. Dictatorship contradicts itself inasmuch as it declares the Christian idea of original sin abolished, frees man of conscience, and teaches him noble heroics (in order to make him a better fighter in its defence), but at the same time degrades and enslaves him without the slightest feeling for his dignity, convinced that he deserves no better fate and that every other attitude is antiquated, sentimental talk. Both are illogical. But which form of illogical thinking is the more decent?

I spoke of the characteristic friendliness of democracy to intellect and also to the arts, to literature; and it is scarcely necessary to add that this, in itself, distinguishes it very definitely from dictatorship, which because of its belief in force is thereby obligated to be remote, foreign, and hostile to intellectual pursuits. But this assertion only acquires real value as a definition of democracy if the concept of intellectual life is not understood as one-sided, isolated, abstract, superior to life and remote from it, but is characterized as closely related to life, as directed toward life and action — for only that and specifically that is the democratic spirit. That is the spirit of democracy. Democracy is not intellectualistic in an old and outworn sense.

Democracy is thought; but it is thought related to life and action. Otherwise it would not be democratic, and herewith I give a definition which contributes to the modernity and the originality of democracy. The French philosopher Bergson sent to a philosophical congress which recently met in Paris a message in which he set up this imperative: " Act as men of thought, think as men of action." That is a thoroughly democratic slogan. No intellectual of the pre-democratic era ever thought of action, nor of what kind of action would result if his thinking were put into practice. It is characteristic of undemocratic or of democratically uneducated nations that their thinking goes on without reference to reality, in pure abstraction, in complete isolation of the mind from life itself, and without the slightest consideration for the realistic consequences of thought. That indicates a lack of pragmatism which is reprehensible. As a result thought meets with a horrible defeat through reality, and thinking, in general, is compromised. Goethe said: " The man of action is always conscienceless; conscience belongs only to the observer." That is true, but because it is true,

the observer must also be conscientious on behalf
of the man of action — a requirement which is of
course most happily fulfilled when both thought
and action reside in one and the same person.

We call the recently deceased founder and first
President of the Czechoslovak Republic a great
democrat. Why? Because he embodied a new and
modern relationship between mind and life, because
he represented the organic association of the philosopher and the statesman — a philosopher as
statesman, and as a statesman a philosopher.
Plato's insistence that philosophers should rule the
state would create a dangerous Utopia if it merely
implied that the ruler should be a philosopher. The
philosopher must also be a ruler — for that, primarily, creates the relationship of mind and life
which we call democratic. What we admire today
in Descartes, the philosopher who stands at the beginning of modern thought, is specifically the prox-
imity to life and action of his mode of thinking; and
the longer European philosophy pursued this democratic trend of thought since that Cartesian era, the
more decisive it became. Even so extremely indi-

vidualistic and aristocratic a thinker as Nietzsche is a democrat in this specifically modern sense; his battle against the theorist, his almost excessive and dangerous glorification of life at the expense of thought and abstract truth, is of a philosophic-democratic character, and of a very artistic one, at that. For the artist is not a theorist, or, at least, only in immediate reference to the kind of action, the creative activity, that arises out of the mind. In more than one way Nietzsche brought art and scientific thinking close together, allowed them to fuse one into the other; through him the borderline between them faded away. But to come close to art means to come close to life, and if an appreciation of the dignity of man is the moral definition of democracy, then its psychological definition arises out of its determination to reconcile and combine knowledge and art, mind and life, thought and deed.

To be sure, misunderstanding and misuse of this concept lie close at hand. There exists a caricature of this modern anti-intellectualism which has nothing whatever to do with democracy, but which lands us in the middle of the base demagogic world of fascism. This is the contempt of pure reason, the denial and violation of truth in favour of power and the interests of the state, the appeal to the lower instincts, to so-called " feeling," the release of stupidity and evil from the discipline of reason and intelligence, the emancipation of blackguardism — in short, a barbaric mob-movement, beside which what we call democracy certainly stands out as aristocratic to the highest degree. In fact, the contrast between democracy and aristocracy is only inadequately justified by life itself; the one is not always the real antithesis of the other. If aristocracy really and always meant " the rule of the good, of the best," then it would be the most desirable of all things because it would be exactly what we understand by democracy. Masaryk the democrat, Roosevelt the democrat, Léon Blum the democrat, are certainly more aristocratic as individual types of men and of statesmen than such types as Hitler or Mussolini, who are both outright plebeians. But it is logical that people of an aristocratic bent should represent the principle of democracy politically, because intellect confers distinction and is in itself an expression of refinement and of a higher category. Moreover, because of its association and solidarity with knowledge, truth, justice, and as the opposite of violence and vulgarity, intellect becomes the advocate and representative of democracy on earth.

Real democracy, as we understand it, can never dispense with aristocratic attributes — if the word " aristocratic " is used, not in the sense of birth or any sort of privilege, but in a spiritual sense. In a democracy which does not respect the intellectual life and is not guided by it, demagogy has free play, and the level of national life is depressed to that of the ignorant and uncultivated. But this cannot happen if the principle of education is allowed to dominate and the tendencies prevail to raise the lower classes to an appreciation of culture and to accept the leadership of the better elements. If the conception of culture and its level are determined from below, according to the ideas and understanding of the mob — this, precisely, is nothing but demagogy; and we have its perfect exemplification in the so-called " *Kultur* " speeches of the above-

mentioned Hitler. One of these speeches had the
practical result that contemporary German painters
of world renown such as Corinth, Kokoschka, Pech-
stein, Klee, Hofer, Marck, and Nolde were figura-
tively and, one might say, personally pilloried.
Their works were exposed in an exhibition of " degenerate art," to the ridicule of those whose greatest
exponent is the same " *Kultur* " orator. The non-
sense which this new kind of ruler talks in an au-
thoritative manner upon art and intellect, upon
sculpture, painting, literature, will make clear to
future generations what could happen in the war-
damaged Germany of our day, a country which once
enjoyed a great intellectual position; it will show
them what " degenerate democracy " is like. I
know nothing about the art of government — it is
possible that this zealot is leading Germany toward
a glorious future, although William II also prom-
ised that. But on the subject of culture I am somewhat at home. That I can legitimately discuss.
And since Germany is wrapped in the funereal si-
lence of dictatorship, since there all opposition is
choked, human dignity demands that, at least, here

in freedom it should be asserted that these " *Kultur* " orations are nothing but low and vulgar babble and that their only value is to prove how democracy degenerates when it loses the necessary influences of intellectual leadership.

To be sure, pseudo-aristocratic pretensions play a part in this degeneracy. Dictators are lordly creatures, they despise the masses, and while they make themselves the mouthpiece of vulgar opinion, they let the masses understand what seems incomprehensible and unjustified — namely, that they have nothing but contempt for them. The people, says the *Kultur* orator, must be silent; it needs bread and circuses, and that's that. The people have a " rabbit horizon " and are made up chiefly of " weak philistines." But in reality the mob mind prevails in and through the leader, and it is truly amazing to behold how it never occurs to this ruling orator that there is any relationship between his cultural views and a " rabbit horizon " or " weak philistinism." This is what I call pseudo-aristocracy — in a fascist dictatorship everything is " pseudo," especially its socialism, as the attitude of the *Kultur* orator toward the people clearly demonstrates. It is a socialism marked by human contempt, by the antipathy to culture characteristic of provincials. All in all, it is a bolshevism of the ignoble, which undoubtedly is a more horrible danger to civilization than the social doctrines whose menace has driven so many of the propertied classes into the arms of fascism or at any rate inspires them with sympathy for it. They consider fascism a protective bulwark which will save them from the real, the Russian, proletarian bolshevism and from socialism in general. The fascist dictatorships actually pretend to be such a protective bulwark, they act the part of saviours of European civilization against bolshevism, toward which, they maintain, democracy is a preliminary step. They can be said to exist by means of this artificially propagated fear; this fear, above everything, helped the fascists to their internal victory and they are confident that the antibolshevist ideology, tirelessly propagandized, will help them to the external or world victory.

But the propertied classes should be warned of the cruel disappointment which awaits them if they yield to this fraudulent propaganda — a great disappointment which the citizens of those countries that have lapsed into fascism have already experienced. The idea that fascism — especially German National-Socialism — has the function and intention to preserve private property and an individualistic society is completely erroneous. In certain respects, particularly economically, National-Socialism is nothing but bolshevism. These two are hostile brothers of whom the younger has learned everything from the older, the Russian, excepting only morality; for German socialism is morally spurious, deceitful, and humanly contemptuous, but in its economic effect it is practically identical with bolshevism. Under National-Socialism, to be sure, the workers are deprived of rights, the unions are destroyed, all socialistic organizations are annihilated. But the hope that this would bring about the golden age of capitalism was a dream of Herr Thyssen and other financial patrons of the Hitler party. The beauty of this dream is open to doubt, but in any case the exact opposite became a reality. The war-economy which now prevails in the Third

The Coming Victory of Democracy

Reich is a morally low form of socialism, but nevertheless a form of it. It is something that could just as well be called state socialism as state capitalism, a military dictatorship of the state over national economy, a complete elimination of business initiative, the unquestionable collapse of private capitalistic economy. The propertied classes of the world should be perfectly clear in their minds about this before they declare themselves in favour of fascism through fear of socialism.

It cannot, moreover, be sufficiently emphasized that fascist socialism is a moral travesty of real socialism, the pillage of a civilized and humanitarian idea in order to exploit it for a propaganda of youthfulness and future glory. The state of mind of socialist dictatorship is clearly illustrated by the exaggerated building program in present-day Germany. The impulse of this regime to glorify itself in luxurious and enormous public buildings that are just as morbidly ambitious as they are artistically wretched, is an obsession of a decidedly abnormal kind. It has something maniacal about it and calls to mind that a building mania is clinically a well-

known symptom. Money plays absolutely no role
in these state and community buildings that are going up everywhere, some of which are only planned,
while others already stand resplendent in their
desolate, empty, and decadent completion. The ex-
penditures involved are enormous; " National turn-
over " seems to permit it.

In Nürnberg — to say nothing of the architec-
tural plans and accomplishments at Berlin and Mu-
nich — a so-called " Temple City " is going up in
which future party congresses are to be celebrated.
A stone sports-arena is being constructed to hold
404,000 people, which will be four times as big
as the Olympic stadium in Berlin; also an enormous auditorium which, seen from the back, re-
sembles the Roman Colosseum — how it will look
in front, I cannot say. A special giant structure for
" *Kultur* meetings " is also included, apparently
richly adorned with columns which will shelter a
type of *Kultur* that can readily be imagined. The
" Zeppelin field " near Nürnberg is big enough to
serve as a setting for the annual war games of the
defensive forces, with tanks and heavy artillery.

But that is not enough. A parade-ground three times as big, surrounded by stone walls, is in preparation which is called by the Cæsarian name of "March field." This will hold a million people. If one considers that the Berlin "Reich sports-field" cost fifty million marks, one can approximately guess what the "March field" and especially the Nürnberg "Temple City" — to speak only of these — will consume. And at the same time the direst housing shortage exists in Germany — a direct result of this large-scale construction mania, as can be readily understood. Based on official figures, it has been estimated that there is a shortage of 950,000 homes in the nation. The spectacle of the Reich's magnificence as represented by these monster structures must compensate the homeless and the badly housed.

And that is called socialism! It is National-Socialism, let it be remembered. But I consider it more national and also more socially minded when President Roosevelt approaches the American Congress with a plan for the construction of three or four million new homes, the cost of which — and they

Thomas Mann

are high costs — will be met jointly by private enterprise and federal subsidies. Magnificence is by no means absent from such planning. But it is a magnificence which is not designed to dazzle and intimidate people through a grand and glorious expansion of the regime, but which is aimed at the needs and the reasonable well-being of the population.

The word " socialism " is a lie when used by the fascists in spite of all the appearances of an anti-individualistic economy. This is indicated by the German version of the name: National-Socialism. This combination of words is a deliberate deception, as is the whole field of thought for which it serves as a label. Nationalism and socialism are opposites. To make a party program out of the two is mental dishonesty. Socialism is an entirely moral impulse — which means that it is turned inward, that it is an impulse of conscience. Whatever one may think of socialism from the point of view of economic and political individualism, one must admit that it is peace-loving, pacifist even to the point of endangering itself. From its very nature it has little sense of power — and if it should be destroyed, it will be owing to this deficiency.

Did we not see the socialistically inclined German Republic lay down its weapons before its assassins through pacifist dread of bloodshed, of civil war? We have also seen how much pressure from the aggressive, warlike powers was needed before the French and English socialistic pacifists were able to reconcile themselves out of sheer necessity to the defensive armament program of their countries. That is why I call socialism a moral impulse, because its interests are essentially in internal and not in external politics; its passion is justice, right not might. The socialistic reforms of Léon Blum in France occurred at the almost criminal neglect of foreign policy, in the idealistic belief that the establishment of a higher and just order of things within the country would of itself strengthen it in every respect. This is belief in morality. Although this belief, in spite of its idealism, is in the long run the right one, for the present it can be an enfeebling and dangerous influence in the life-struggle, just as any human being who lives wholly within himself and fastens his attention exclusively upon his own salvation, taking no thought for his environment and his adjustment to it, would in all probability fare badly on earth. And Russia? One may wholly disapprove of the example which it sets for internal politics and fear this example. But it must be admitted that the moral nature of all real socialism is substantiated even in the case of Russia; one must recognize it as a peacefully disposed nation and admit that, as such, it constitutes a reinforcement of democracy. It is not an accident nor a mere question of politics but one of morality if Russia aligns herself with the big and little democracies; England, France, America, Czechoslovakia. When peace is endangered, socialism and bourgeois democracy belong on the same side, for the feeling for peace is an internal problem. It is a human quest of broadest ethical significance, the quest of humanity for its own development. War, on the other hand, is moral indolence, profligate adventure, immature escape from the great and urgent problems of social reform which peace imposes, problems which can only be solved in a state of peace. I have perhaps an insufficient awareness of the menace emanating from Russia toward the capitalistic social order; for I am no capitalist. But at least I can see that Russia does not imperil the essential upon which all else depends — namely, peace. It is not Russia that forces Europe, twenty years after the World War, to withdraw enormous resources from peaceful purposes and apply them to armaments; it is fascism and its so-called dynamics. If the world cannot achieve peace and progress, it is the fault of fascism and not of socialism.

In direct contrast to socialism, nationalism is a thoroughly aggressive impulse, directed against the outer world; its concern is not with conscience, but with power; not with human achievement, but with war. To help the preparations for war and its glorification, the word " socialism " with its great propaganda value is cleverly used. As an actual fact, socialism is being murdered at home. But externally, internationally, there is a sudden pretence of socialism; at once such concepts as " proletarian," " poverty," " wealth," " justice," play a prominent role, and class-warfare, internally denied, abhorred

and replaced by a dubious " national unity," is pro-
jected externally as the dynamic force of all history.
The world is divided, on the one hand, into proletarian nations, the have-nots, with nothing to lose and
everything to win, which are being made dynamic
and heroic through poverty, yearning for space,
sun, happiness, and partnership in the assets of the
earth. And on the other side are the capitalistic
states, satisfied and static, resting upon their pos-
sessions like the treasure-guarding dragon, who
wish to exclude all poor devils from the happiness
and wealth of the world. Socialistic rights and
the pathos of dynamic as opposed to static nations
are used for all they are worth. The overthrow of
present conditions of ownership in favour of the
" poor " is demagogically propagandized and the
capitalistic world is threatened with a proletarian
war if this demand is not satisfied.

Now, as life is constituted, truth depends to some
extent on the man who speaks it. From certain
sources even the truth becomes a lie. There is no
doubt that, among the variations and the emotion-
ally intelligible modifications of the idea — truth,

freedom, justice — it is what we call justice that is closest to the conscience and the heart of humanity today. It is a fact that every alert mentality recognizes in juster social and economic arrangements the challenge of the day, and it is likewise beyond dispute that this vital moral challenge must be extended not only to the inner structure of the state, but also to the community of states and their international relations. Europe and the world are ripe for the consideration of an inclusive reform of the regulation of natural resources and the redistribution of wealth. Naturally this socialization of raw materials must be undertaken as part of a general agreement and of a sensible and mutual solution of conflicts — in short, in the spirit of peace, of progress, and of universal welfare. But it is unfortunately true that precisely those countries which are now propagandizing externally for justice are the least prepared for this idea — are, in fact, morally unequal to it. They utter their cry for justice only out of national egoism that is naked and unadulterated, and nothing is further removed from their thought than the realization that they, too, must make sacrifices for the general welfare. If such a thing is suggested to them, if it is proposed that they make some sort of concession to the collective understanding and pacification, they at once talk contemptuously of a " political barter " to which they cannot possibly lend their name. They wish only to take, not to give. Not for the sake of peace and common progress do they demand the reorganization of wealth, but to increase their power, to give additional strength to their war threats, and, in case of war, to be able to conduct it successfully.

Evidently the " external socialism " of the fascist dictatorships is not exactly the right kind. It has, necessarily, as little reality as the internal variety. It is a lie, for its purpose is to distract attention from internal moral and social problems to which a decent government that is genuinely considerate of the welfare, the honour, and the happiness of its people, one that is not merely thinking of the preservation of its power and of intimidating its subjects through external triumphs, would be obliged to give its chief attention. Today the pacifism of nations who desire peace and have the right to use this word rests upon the insight that war is no longer admissible, that Europe has arrived at a stage of social maturity in which war has become impossible as a political weapon. These nations realize that peace sets humanity its problems to-day, and that these problems are big and urgent enough to absorb the whole energy and intelligence, all the capacity for self-sacrifice, and all the courage of mankind. War is nothing but a cowardly escape from the problems of peace. It substitutes external adventure for internal effort and improvement, and it has fallen so deeply into moral disrepute because it now stands revealed for what it has always been, a means of internal oppression, of keeping the populace in subjection, the great and perfidious means of getting them to shout " Hurrah " over their own defeat at the hands of their triumphant rulers. The contrast of nationalism and socialism is defined by the contrast of war and peace. A " glorious," externally successful regime need no longer concern itself with internal improvements. It frees itself of all responsibility for problems of culture and progress when it stands forth in the splendour of military victories, and the populace, dazzled and stupefied by this splendour, screams: " Hurrah! " Does anyone believe that Abyssinia was conquered — or occupied — for the great happiness of the Italian people and not to support the tottering power of the fascist regime? This was the reason why the Abyssinian villages had to be fumigated with poisonous gases in the greatest haste.

Inversely, a government that is hostile to freedom and peace avoids war not out of concern for the evils that it may conjure up for its people, but exclusively through fear of weakening or destroying its authority in case of defeat. It weighs its *own* chances of victory, not those of the people. This is the false pacifism of states inimical to freedom. Such states neither keep peace nor make war to enhance the happiness and honour of their people. Both possibilities are carefully weighed as to the support that each would give toward maintaining the reign of terror at home. The socialistic-proletarian grimace which they make externally has no other purpose. It is a silly lie. If these countries are overpopulated, why do their rulers strive by every means for an increase of the birth-rate, for an expansion of the population that strains their resources still more? It is boldly unmoral to call the demand for expansion socialistic until the right to make such a claim has been earned through internal colonization and through decent agricultural reform measures. Instead of deciding in favour of a peace policy that would be real and genuine, and not merely inspired by the fear of their own downfall; instead of adapting themselves to a socially collective system which would result in a flourishing world trade, in an exchange of strength and achievement and in mutual assistance — in short, in all the blessings of reason — these states pursue autarchy, isolation, war-economy, and the artificial elimination of unemployment through armament-production, whereby they force the rest of the world to transform itself into a similar military encampment and prevent the other nations from devoting themselves to the problems of peace. And yet, despite all this, they have the audacity to pretend that they are great socialists.

I stated, ladies and gentlemen, that faith in the

ultimate victory of democracy over its adversaries, and this victory itself, depend upon certain conditions whose historical fulfilment is now incumbent upon democracy. I mentioned the first of these conditions; it is democracy's deep and forceful recollection of itself, the renewal of its spiritual and moral self-consciousness, the release through thought and feeling of that youthfulness which springs from its humanity and its timelessness. The second condition will be fulfilled through the clear and frank appreciation of the unquestionable practical and menacing advantages upon which democracy's momentary opponent and rival, dictatorial fascism, bases its hopes of victory. It would be useless to deny the superiority which the dictatorial system derives from its aggressive foreign policy, dearly as it is being paid for, and from its firm will-power, which may be merely simulated, may indeed very often be wholly fictitious, but which is effective even as a pretence since the system knows ways and means of imposing it not only upon the other nations but, primarily, upon its own people. What we think we are, that to a certain extent we actually become. Such a nation actually appears to be — at least momentarily — a united, extremely self-conscious and active body politic, harmonious in itself and well co-ordinated, steeled through an economic war-asceticism, which is felt, it must be conceded, not exclusively as pressure and deprivation but also as an incitement, as cause for pride, and as a great national adventure. The happiness, the freedom, even the life of the individual count for nothing. He is a citizen of the state and nothing else, an atom of the nation that embodies the state. He is obliged — at first by force, which, however, gradually takes hold of the inner man as well — to devote his thought, feeling, will, and deeds, first and last, to the totality, and to serve it with body and soul, with all that he has and all that he is. To the achievement of an ascetic-heroic military efficiency and future grandeur, the totalitarian state subordinates every phase of public life with an iron hand. It would not be totalitarian if it permitted any kind of life to escape its control and its service. That is not permitted even to the most intimate and private recesses of the soul. What we call culture — re-

ligion, art, research, higher morality, free human
thought — not only does not count but falls under
the crime of treason to the extent that it claims any
sort of freedom or individual dignity.

Democracy as a whole is still far from acquiring
a clear conception of this fascist concentration, of
the fanaticism and absolutism of the totalitarian
state. It willingly sacrifices all culture and humanity for the sake of power and victory, and secures
for itself in this unfair way advantages and ad-
vances in the battle of life such as have never been
seen before, whose effect upon civilization is wholly
bewildering. And yet, in order to be able to survive, democracy must understand this new thing in
all of its thoroughly vicious novelty. Democracy's
danger is the humane illusion, the virtuous belief
that compromise with this new creature is possible,
that it can be won over to the idea of peace and collective reconstruction by forbearance, friendliness,
or amicable concessions. That is a dangerous mis-
take which is founded on the wholly different
thought-process of the democratic and of the fascist mentality. Democracy and fascism live, so

to speak, on different planets, or, to put it more
accurately, they live in different epochs. The fascist interpretation of the world and of history is one
of absolute force, wholly free of morality and reason and having no relation to them. Its demands
cannot be satisfied and quieted with concessions, but
are thoroughly vague, indefinable, and boundless.
The thoughts of democracy and fascism cannot
meet because the latter is deeply and unquali-
fiedly involved in the concept of power and hegemony as the aim and substance of politics, at a
period when democracy is no longer interested in
power and hegemony, nor in politics as a means
toward gaining them, but is interested only in peace.
It is a conflict of misunderstanding, actually con-
taining considerable historical comedy, but undoubtedly providing vital dangers for democracy.
Certain as it may be to us that a system which has
given up the thought of power politics and has, so
to speak, discovered peace, represents the higher,
later, newer stage of development of mind and
morals, just so convinced is fascism of its own vitality and future and of the backwardness, decrepi-

tude, and historical weakness of democracy. In every friendly gesture, in every concession to its demands, it will always see only a sign of weakness, of resignation, and of timely abdication.

As for Germany, it is both too soon and too late for a sympathetic recognition of its demands. It would have been reasonable to meet Germany halfway before National-Socialism came into power, when a peace-loving German Republic was to be supported and protected against fascism. Such a meeting of German demands will again be in order after Hitler's fall. But for the present any yielding to Nazi threats means a cruel and discouraging blow to those forces within the German people that are sincerely working toward freedom and peace; and since German demands that issue from National-Socialism are never aimed at peace, but exclusively at an increase of power and the improvement of its military position, their fulfilment does not serve peace but war.

It is necessary that democracy should understand this. It must also understand the advantages which fascism derives from a world situation in which the distinction between war and peace is wiped out and neither the one nor the other distinctly prevails. It is scarcely possible to maintain that peace exists and yet no declaration of war has been issued; an official and undeclared war is being waged, as an experiment, in remote places with limited means while the big war apparatus is still being carefully saved up — an equivocal or, at least, not a very explicit situation which fascism has discovered and in which it feels very much at home. It is probable that fascism will continue to prefer this kind of war to actual open warfare as long as possible, for a real war would soon reveal the important role which lies and deception play in the " totalitarian state." The repressed forces of human freedom would undoubtedly be released at the first reverse which tyranny suffered. That is why fascism avoids the war to which it educates its own people, while it delivers its pacifist opponents to the executioner's sword. In reality, fascism seriously doubts that its national unity could endure the supreme ordeal of war if it were to last any length of time. A revealing statement was made by a German staff officer in which he spoke of the three fronts on which the coming war would have to be waged: on land, in the air, and at home. That is significant. Fascism admits that, in case of war, not the least of its difficulties would be created by its own people and its own nation; that it is by no means certain whether the people would follow it through thick and thin; that, on the contrary, an external war will almost immediately mean civil war as well. No wonder that it prefers peace to such a risk, or rather that condition between peace and war which is its own invention. For this permits fascism to continue its internal and external bluff with greater impunity, to blackmail the peace-loving democracies and perhaps to achieve its ambitions for power without an actual war, especially if it uses the time gained in this way for a type of political strategy in relation to which democracy finds itself as good as helpless, for reasons, it must be admitted, that are humanly sympathetic — namely, because the moral tone of the democracies does not permit them to reply in kind. It is the lowest kind of politics, smelling of the dime novel and of criminality, highly repulsive to look upon, and proof of how political action degenerates when the will and spirit of the world have outgrown such behaviour, and " politics " are conducted only in a backward and anachronistic manner. Murder, bribery, corrupt intrigue play the principal role. Such methods are of unrestrained baseness, but for the time being they are of undeniable effectiveness, if the adversary for reasons of decency is obliged to stand with arms folded while such things run their course.

I am picturing conditions, ladies and gentlemen, which will painfully delay that triumph of democracy in which we all believe, and which can place serious historical defeats in democracy's path if it does not clearly realize the situation and meet it with all of its innate resources of vitality and re-invigoration. Let me try to state simply what is needed. A reform of freedom is necessary which will make of it something very different from the freedom that existed and could exist in the times of our fathers and grandfathers, the epoch of bourgeois liberalism. Now we need something different from " laissez-faire, laissez-aller," for freedom cannot survive on such a basis. It is no longer adequate. The reform I have in mind must be a social reform, a reform in the social sense. Only in this way can democracy take the wind out of the sails of fascism and also of bolshevism and overcome the merely temporary and deceptive advantages which the charm of novelty gives the dictatorships. Moreover, this social reform must aim at spiritual as well as economic freedom. In both directions the times of Manchesterism and of passive liberalism are gone forever. Freedom has been driven out of liberalism — driven out by deepest anguish. But liberalism has learned its lesson. Humanity will no longer mean a tolerance that endures everything — even the determination to destroy humanity. Face to face with fanaticism incarnate, a freedom which through sheer goodness and humane scepticism no longer believes in itself will be irrevocably lost. It is not the sort of humanity which is weak and patient to the point of self-doubt that freedom needs today. Such an attitude makes freedom look pathetic and contemptible in the face of a power-concept which is not in the least sicklied o'er with the pale cast of thought. What is needed is a humanity strong in will and firm in the determination to preserve itself. Freedom must discover its virility. It must learn to walk in armour and to defend itself against its deadly enemies. And after the most bitter experiences, it must finally understand that a pacifism which admits it will not wage war under any circumstances will surely bring about war instead of banishing it.

So much for the spiritual reform of freedom. As to its renewal from the economic point of view, one can only say what everybody knows, that its moral defect and disadvantage which actually permits fascism to play itself up as " idealistic " is its plutocratic aspect, which was established by the bourgeois revolution as a more modern but not more worthy substitute for feudal privileges and inequalities. If democracy wishes to make its undoubted moral superiority over fascism effective and challenge its pseudo-socialism, it must adopt in the economic as well as the spiritual domain as much of socialistic morality as the times make imperative and indispensable. Here, likewise, freedom must be restored through social discipline. Democracy must continue to develop the bourgeois revolution not only politically but also economically. For justice is the dominant idea of this epoch, and its realization, as far as is humanly possible, has become a matter of world conscience, from which there is no escape and which can no longer be neglected. It is ridiculous, for example, to see Franco, the General of the Spanish reaction, make socialistic promises to the population which is desperately resisting his revolt. What is the use of this enterprise begun on behalf of feudalism, capitalism, and foreign influences, why have a civil war at all, if his only aim is to establish socialism? But, of course, we know how the word is used — in the fascist sense. This good enemy of the people never dreamed that he would ever so much as speak the word, but his German and Italian advisers, who understand fascist propaganda, have told him that nothing can be done today without it. This, in itself, proves what a dominant position is assigned to social concepts by the spirit of the times. Everybody who would consider it a great human disaster

if, in this historical struggle of the world philoso-
phies, democracy should succumb for lack of adapt-
ability, must desire as one desires a necessity that
liberal democracy will develop into social democracy, from the economic as well as the spiritual
point of view.

Is this demand alarming because it sounds revolutionary? Its revolutionary nature must be taken
in a relative sense. In reality its implications are
conservative, for it aims to preserve our Occidental
cultural traditions, to defend them against barbarism and political running amuck of every sort. I
call Franklin D. Roosevelt a conservative statesman
just because of the social bent which he gives to
democracy. He is a true friend and a genuine serv-
ant of liberty even when he limits and regulates it
socialistically, for it is by such means that he takes
the wind out of the sails of fascism and bolshevism
alike. For the same reason I call the endeavours of
the French popular front conservative, and in doing
so find myself in agreement with such political
conservatives as the Catholic deputy Le Cour Grand-
Maison, who in addition is also a royalist, and who

Thomas Mann

is considered one of the most important personalities in the French Chamber. " Let us hope," he said recently, " that the day will soon dawn when Frenchmen without distinction of social origin will find themselves united upon a new basis and will put into effect in the interest of France and of freedom what is called a structural reform by some people, and what I myself will call a peaceful revolution. It is not our duty to preserve an inhuman social order, but, on the contrary, every effort must be made to establish in its place a more humane order which will create a true hierarchy of values, put money in the service of production, production in the service of humanity, and humanity itself in the service of an ideal which gives meaning to life." These are the words of a Christian conservative representative of a country which in social considerations is the most sensitive on earth. They are new words. They express what is new in contemporary thinking. This idea, so new to our world, is what the political youth of France calls " economic humanism." " What is really new in our world," said the Belgian Vandervelde in answer to the Condottiere of the Palazzo

The Coming Victory of Democracy

Venezia when he was again prophesying that all Europe would become fascist by tomorrow, " what is essentially and actually new in the world is social democracy."

That is the truth. It is this truth that freedom, rejuvenated by the resources of its timelessness, opposes to the boastful pretensions to youthfulness made by dictatorship. The social renewal of democracy is the presupposition and the guarantee of its victory. This renewal will create a national unity which will prove itself far superior to the tissue of falsehoods which fascism calls by that name. In democracy this communal spirit is already a living force. For this is the aim of all political action — the community of nations — and this eventually will abolish politics itself.

I am aware, ladies and gentlemen, that today's lecture had to be a trifle theoretical, in its attempt to define the exalted and comprehensive concept of democracy. And so I feel certain that you will forgive me if in conclusion I say a few words of a personal nature. I do not know how many of you are familiar with my written works. I am no sansculotte, no Jacobin, no revolutionary — my whole being is that of a conservative; that is to say that I stand by tradition. I am a man who regards it as his task in life to advance the German heritage, though with modern means and in the modern spirit; who, if his friends are to be believed, may hope one day to assume a place in the history of German culture. No one, I am sure, will interpret anything I have said as a desire to destroy cultural values. I left Germany because in the Germany of today the traditional values underlying Western culture have been rejected and trodden under foot. I have made many sacrifices in order to save one thing which was denied me in Germany: freedom of thought and expression. What better use could I make of this freedom than to tell of my experience during my last years in Germany and what it taught me.

To me the chief lesson of those years is that we must not be afraid to attempt a reform of freedom — in the conservative sense. I believe it to be the duty of every thinking man to take an active part in this task — which is tantamount to the preservation of culture — and to give freely of himself. I must regretfully own that in my younger years I shared that dangerous German habit of thought which regards life and intellect, art and politics as totally separate worlds. In those days we were all of us inclined to view political and social matters as nonessentials that might as well be entrusted to politicians. And we were foolish enough to rely on the ability of these specialists to protect our highest interests. Not long after the war, however, I recognized the threat to liberty which was beginning to take form in Germany, and almost alone among writers I warned the public to the best of my powers. When subsequently the spectre became reality and National-Socialism achieved absolute power, I realized at once that I should not be able to breathe in this air, that I should have to leave my home. In Switzerland, one of Europe's oldest democracies, I found an honourable haven, for which I am duly grateful. Even more do I owe thanks to the Republic of Czechoslovakia, which most generously made a gift of its citizenship to me who was robbed of my German nationality. Especially at this moment, when the heavens of central Europe are darkening so threateningly, it is a heartfelt necessity to give expression to my faithful loyalty to this courageous and lovable democratic republic.

Four years ago I visited America for the first time, and since then I have come here each year. I was delighted with the atmosphere that I found here, because it was almost free of the poisons that fill the air of Europe — because here, in contrast to the cultural fatigue and inclination to barbarism prevalent in the Old World, there exists a joyful respect for culture, a youthful sensitivity to its values and its products. I feel that the hopes of all those who cherish democratic sentiments in the sense in which I have defined them, must be concentrated on this country. Here it will be possible — here it *must* be possible — to carry out those reforms of which I have spoken; to carry them out by peaceful labour, without crime and bloodshed. It is my own intention to make my home in your country, and I am convinced that if Europe continues for a while to pursue the same course as in the last two decades, many good Europeans will meet again on American soil. I believe, in fact, that for the duration of the present European dark age, the centre of Western culture will shift to America. America has received much from Europe, and that debt will be amply repaid if, by saving our traditional values from the present gloom, she can preserve them for a brighter future that will once again find Europe and America united in the great tasks of humanity.

American Editions of the Works of
THOMAS MANN

ROYAL HIGHNESS. *Translated by* A. Cecil Curtis. 1916. (out of print)

BUDDENBROOKS. *Translated by* H. T. Lowe-Porter. 1924

DEATH IN VENICE AND OTHER STORIES.* *Translated by* Kenneth Burke. 1925

THE MAGIC MOUNTAIN. *Translated by* H. T. Lowe-Porter. 1927

CHILDREN AND FOOLS.* *Translated by* Herman George Scheffauer. 1928

THREE ESSAYS. *Translated by* H. T. Lowe-Porter. 1929

EARLY SORROW.* *Translated by* Herman George Scheffauer. 1930

A MAN AND HIS DOG.* *Translated by* Herman George Scheffauer. 1930

DEATH IN VENICE.** *A new translation by* H. T. Lowe-Porter, *with an Introduction by* Ludwig Lewisohn. 1930

MARIO AND THE MAGICIAN.** *Translated by* H. T. Lowe-Porter. 1931

* These stories are now included, in translations by Mrs. Lowe-Porter, in *Stories of Three Decades.*
** Now included in *Stories of Three Decades.*

Bibliography

PAST MASTERS AND OTHER PAPERS. *Translated by* H. T. Lowe-Porter. 1933. (out of print)

JOSEPH AND HIS BROTHERS. *I. Joseph and His Brothers. 1934. II. Young Joseph. 1935. III (two volumes). Joseph in Egypt. 1938. Translated by* H. T. Lowe-Porter

STORIES OF THREE DECADES. *Translated by* H. T. Lowe-Porter. 1936

AN EXCHANGE OF LETTERS. *Translated by* H. T. Lowe-Porter. 1937

FREUD, GOETHE, WAGNER. *Translated by* H. T. Lowe-Porter and Rita Matthias-Reil. 1937